For Sage, Maya, and Ezra.
You are fearfully and wonderfully made. May
you all come to love and serve the God who
created you in His image for His glory.

New Growth Press, Greensboro, NC 27404
Text Copyright © 2018 by Shai Linne
Illustration Copyright © 2018 by Trish Mahoney

Art and Design: Trish Mahoney

ISBN: 978-1-948130-13-4 (Print)
ISBN: 978-1-948130-14-1 (eBook)

Library of Congress Cataloging-in-Publication Data on file
Printed in China
25 24 23 22 21 20 19 18 1 2 3 4 5

GOD MADE
ME AND YOU

Celebrating God's Design for Ethnic Diversity

Shai Linne

Illustrated by
Trish Mahoney

"After this I looked, and behold, a great multitude that no one could number, from every nation, from all tribes and peoples and languages, standing before the throne and before the Lamb, clothed in white robes, with palm branches in their hands, and crying out with a loud voice, 'Salvation belongs to our God who sits on the throne, and to the Lamb!'"

Revelation 7:9–10

Dear Parent or Caregiver,

Thank you for taking the time to read *God Made Me AND You* to your child. This book was written to help you teach your child about the beauty of God's design for diversity in His image-bearers, with a particular focus on ethnic diversity.

I wrote this little book because I am convinced from Scripture that ethnic diversity is not something that should be begrudgingly tolerated but rather enthusiastically celebrated! Passages like Revelation 7:9-10 speak very loudly to God's ultimate purpose in the gospel—a redeemed, ethnically diverse people worshiping God together for all eternity.

God was intentional in the ways He made us to differ from each other. Like the facets of a jewel, the glory of God shines all the more brightly as the light of His gospel is reflected through different vessels. Conversely, God has determined that without ethnic diversity, we lose the ability to see God shine in particular ways that would have only been possible had there been diversity (Ephesians 2:14-19).

Sadly, in the realm of ethnicity, sin has done what it usually does. It has taken something meant to glorify God and distorted it. The sins of racism, bigotry, and ethnic pride have manifested themselves in many ways in our racially-charged culture, both historically and in the present day. These social sins are learned by children, often from family members, media, or peers.

The gospel offers us a new way. Not just for us, but for our children. When the Lord Jesus stretched out His hands on the cross, He did it not only with particular people in mind, but with particular people groups in mind (Revelation 7:9). The Son of God is so glorious, nothing less than the nations would suffice as His chosen community of worshipers. As Christians, we have the privilege of participating in what God is doing in redemptive history! We also have the responsibility to teach our children this kingdom perspective. Countercultural, biblical views don't just happen. They must be taught.

I pray that the Lord will use this book to help all who read it see the purposeful beauty in how God made us all different, and that it would lead to a lifelong embrace and pursuit of ethnic diversity for the glory of God.

Grace and peace,
Shai

Our story begins on a typical day
in Bible class after recess and play.
The children are there, but Ms. Preston is late.
They're talking and laughing out loud as they wait.

Aa Bb Cc Dd Ee Ff Gg Hh Ii Jj Kk Ll Mm Nn

TODAY'S LESSON

ACTS 17

Oo Pp Qq Rr Ss Tt Uu Vv Ww Xx Yy Zz

GRACE

CHRISTIAN
SCHOOL

Two of the boys
were not too polite,
They teased other kids
with all of their might.

They teased one boy
for the clothes he would wear,
And one poor girl,
they made fun of her hair.
One boy cried
when they laughed at his skin,
It was just at that moment,
Ms. Preston walked in!

"I'm sorry I'm late...
Hey, what's going on?
And why are you crying, Todd?
Tell me what's wrong!"

Todd didn't speak up,
but Abigail Moore
told Ms. Preston
what happened moments before.

After she learned
what the children had witnessed,
She told the two boys
to ask for forgiveness.

Then she spoke to the class, "Now kids, listen here.
I've said it before, but I'll make myself clear.

GRACE

CHRISTIAN
SCHOOL

RULES

1. Respect others
2. Be kind
3. Listen
4. Follow directions

**All God's creatures
must be respected.**

**Bullying of any kind
won't be accepted.**

It's a privilege for you to attend this school,
You will be expelled if you can't keep this rule!"

"Don't be afraid
to ask me any questions,
But let's start with how
this relates to our lesson.

We're in Acts,
following Paul the Apostle
As he travels through Greece,
proclaiming the gospel.

Acts 17, in the 26th verse,
Says 'God made from one man
each nation on earth.'

What that means is we all have the same origin,
Wherever we're born, we come from the same kin.
Though many people find this hard to believe,
Our very first parents were Adam and Eve.

**To bring many from one is what God decided—
In this way, the whole human race is united."**

"When God created the heavens and earth,
He did it to show off His glory and worth.

In Genesis 1, what we see in each verse
Is God made a world that is REALLY diverse.

**The sun and the moon,
the planets and stars,
Saturn and Jupiter,
Venus and Mars—**

Each one is different…
Class, why did God make this?
He made it to show off
His beauty and greatness:

From icebergs to insects,
tornadoes to trees;
From lions to lizards,
flamingos to fleas.

Each in their own way,
their God they are praising.
Their differences cry out,
'God is amazing!'"

"But the crown jewel of the work of His hand
Are those made in His image, both woman and man.

And just as two snowflakes
are never the same,
Each person is different,
unique in their frame.

God made us all—
each kind and each sort;
He made some people tall
and some people short.

He gave some curly hair
while others have straight.
It pleased God to fashion
each wonderful trait.

Brown eyes and green eyes,
hazel and blue,
Each in their own way
works of art we can view.

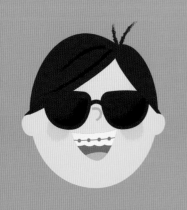

Some that are deaf
and some that are blind
All have great worth
in God's sovereign design."

You were wondrously made in the womb by God's hand.
You are no accident; you are part of His plan.

Rachel and Billy; Keisha, Abigail, Todd—
You're wonderfully made in the image of God.

Carlos, Jennifer, Tyler, Sean, Corey—
God made you; you exist for His glory."

"But back in the garden
with Adam and Eve,
The serpent appeared
with intent to deceive.

They ate from the tree
that God had forbidden,
From that point on,
from their eyes God was hidden.

The sin in each human
would soon be discovered
When Cain, the first-born son,
hated his brother.

Because of their sin, the world was now cursed,
And people's behavior would only get worse.

And now, because
of the presence of sin,
People hate for silly things
like color of skin.

The very differences meant
to give God praise
Are now reasons for hatred,
so evil our ways."

"But God already had
a solution in mind,

HE SENT JESUS

to die for the sins of mankind.

At the cross, we see
what God's love is about,
There's no type of person
that Jesus left out.

Because Jesus died
and rose from the grave,
All those who trust
in the Lord will be saved.

And since that time,
what the Spirit has done
Is drawn many to God
through faith in His Son.

All over the world,
God is filling up churches
With saints of all colors
that Jesus has purchased.

God turns strangers
into sisters and brothers,
Though different, we're called
to love one another."

Спасибо!
(Spasibo!)

Merci!

ありがと
(Arigato!)

"In the book of Revelation, chapter seven,
The church from all times is gathered in heaven.

A great multitude
that no one could number
Praise God with voices
louder than thunder.

Thank you!

Each tribe, each people,
each language, each nation,
All thanking God
for the gift of salvation!

شكرا
(Shukran!)

¡Gracias!

Mahalo!

Ngiyabonga!

There's no sin in heaven,
no hating each other,
Just love from the heart
for our sisters and brothers.

We'll no longer view
our distinctions as odd,
But rather, more reasons
to give praise to God.

Together forever
with saints of all kinds
This is exactly
what God has designed."

"Our lesson's almost over;
it won't be long.
Let's finish our time
by singing this song:"

There's no sin in heaven,
no hating each other,
Just love from the heart
for our sisters and brothers.

We'll no longer view
our distinctions as odd,
But rather, more reasons
to give praise to God.

Together forever
with saints of all kinds
This is exactly
what God has designed."

"Our lesson's almost over;
it won't be long.
Let's finish our time
by singing this song:"

Though we all have a different story
God made me and you, God made me and you
For our joy and for His glory
God made me and you, God made me and you

Different colors and different shades
All fearfully and wonderfully made
Through each, the glory of God displayed
God made me and you

Though all are valued, all are lost
All have great need for the cross
Jesus died, rose, and paid the cost
God made me and you

Though we all have a different story
God made me and you, God made me and you
For our joy and for His glory
God made me and you, God made me and you

Six Ways to Help Your Child Appreciate God's Design for Ethnic Diversity

1. Teach your children what the Bible says about ethnic diversity.

The Bible is not silent when it comes to God's design for ethnic diversity. Embedded in the gospel is God's plan to reconcile to Himself a people from every ethnic group in the world! The bride of Christ is a beautiful, multicolored bride. It's important for us to teach our children these Scripture-based truths. One familiar passage that speaks to the glorious multiethnic future of the church is Revelation 5:9:

"And they sang a new song, saying, 'Worthy are you to take the scroll and to open its seals, for you were slain, and by your blood you ransomed people for God from every tribe and language and people and nation.'"

Every tribe. Every language. Every people. Every nation (*ethnos* in Greek). God's purpose is crystal clear. A diverse people, ransomed for the sake of His praise and glory. We must teach this to our children. And we must stress that the goal of multi-ethnic worship is not only for heaven, we must pursue it now. Here are some passages that will help reinforce this truth. Use them as you talk to your children about how the Spirit draws people from every tribe and nation to worship God:

Genesis 17:4; Numbers 12:1-8; Psalms 22:27-28; 72:11; Daniel 7:14; John 4:9; Acts 10:34-35; 13:47; Romans 15:8-12; Galatians 3:28; Ephesians 2:13-16; James 2:8-9; and Revelation 7:9

2. Correct commonly held errors regarding the Bible and ethnicity for your children.

In Western culture, it is common for literature and films to depict biblical stories that present the characters (and Jesus) as Caucasian, or white. This reinforces the notion that white is normal and non-white is "other." This is particularly dangerous in spiritual matters, where ethnic identity can be mistakenly connected with favor before God. Parents can help their children by pointing out that these illustrations are not accurate depictions of people in the Middle East, where darker features are the norm. Correcting these things will provide opportunities for further dialogue which can be used to help shape your child's worldview.

3. Educate yourself and your children about cultures other than your own.

I'm speaking particularly to white readers. For many white people, especially in the U.S., it is possible to go one's entire life without ever having meaningful interactions with people of color. Additionally, it is all too common for curricula in our schools to focus on Western civilization and accomplishments; again reinforcing the notion that "whiteness" is normative. When people of color are mentioned, it's often limited to depictions of slavery and subservience. Gaining a better understanding of other cultures will take intentionality. The good news is that we're in the information age, with volumes of resources available within seconds of searching the internet.

4. Seek out interactions/relationships with people of different ethnicities.

One of the greatest barriers to pursuing God's design for diversity is the lack of proximity many have with people of different ethnic backgrounds. Depending on where you live, it may take more intentionality in order to develop these relationships. The local church is an ideal context for this pursuit. Unfortunately, there is too much truth in the old saying that "11 a.m. on Sundays is the most segregated hour of the week." If there is ethnic diversity in your church, be intentional about having dinner/family outings/activities with people of different ethnicities so that these kinds of interactions would be the norm, rather than the exception for your child.

Outside of church, it may mean signing your child up for extracurricular activities where they can develop diverse friendships with other children. Sports clubs, choirs, and summer camps can provide these opportunities. Some will have to be more creative than others in this regard.

5. Model loving confrontation of prejudiced words and/or behavior with your children.

Ethnic bigotry certainly spreads from parents who transfer these mind-sets to their children. But often, it comes not from the parents directly, but other family members who may say racially insensitive or even directly racist things in front of the children while the parents passively do nothing. It may not even be a family member. Perhaps it's something said on television. Whatever the case may be, these are opportunities for parents to jump in and say things like, "That joke was not funny. We're all made in God's image and we shouldn't say things like that about other people." or "We love Uncle Bob, but what he said tonight at dinner about other races was unacceptable and sinful. We are to love and accept everyone, regardless of their ethnicity because that's how God loves us." It will require courage to do so, as you may risk alienating a family member. But whatever it may cost relationally, it's worth it for your child to see you honoring God in this way. And it's also the kind of thing that children don't forget.

6. Be hopeful for a future where the Spirit will break down barriers between people of different ethnic backgrounds.

Let your children know through your words, attitudes, and actions that you believe that God is at work in our world, drawing His people to Himself and making us one in answer to His prayer (John 17:20-26). Yes, there is work to do, but the Spirit of the living God is our partner, our helper, and our power. What we can't do in our own strength, God can and will do. Pray with your children through John 17 and then talk with them about how your family can live out Jesus's prayer in your church, school, and neighborhood.

"*God Made Me and You* by Shai Linne is a theologically sound resource for parents and teachers to raise a new generation who will honor God's gift of human diversity. With his poetic gift, Shai wonderfully displays the glory of God right where we need to see it afresh—in how he made me and you!"
Ray Ortlund, Author; pastor of Immanuel Church, Nashville, TN

"Shai Linne poetically guides us through the biblical pattern of creation, fall, redemption, and glorification, unfolding the grand story of the Bible. As he reveals each step in bite-sized chunks, he also teaches the character of an infinitely creative God—One who delights in building a diverse and set-apart people to live with him forever. This is a great addition to every child's bookshelf."
K. A. Ellis, Cannada Fellow for World Christianity, Reformed Theological Seminary

"We read this book to our four daughters. They loved it, and so did we! It's biblically driven, pastorally careful, lyrically beautiful, and, frankly, just inspiring. Use this book to establish good foundations for your children in how to think about God's plan for diversity, and then to praise him for it."
Jonathan and Shannon Leeman, Author; editorial director of 9Marks; elder at Cheverly Baptist Church, Cheverly, MD

"Shai Linne's new book, *God Made Me and You: Celebrating God's Design for Ethnic Diversity*, is a gift. It teaches kids that God making people different is something we can delight in, not fear. More importantly, it shows how our differences are for the purpose of magnifying Jesus, who died to save all kinds of people. Beautifully illustrated and creatively written, I can't wait to read this to my grandkids."
Bob Kauflin, Director of Sovereign Grace Music

"The first time I heard Shai Linne's song 'Penelope Judd,' I knew he had a beautiful father's heart and a keen ability to communicate deep ideas in simple ways to children. *God Made Me and You* applies these gifts to the vitally important topic of race. It is biblically grounded, and therefore God- and gospel-centered, and provides a joyful and unifying perspective on a divisive topic. I want every child and adult I know to read this book!"
Erik Thoennes, Professor at Biola University; author of *Life's Biggest Questions: What the Bible Says about the Things That Matter*

"*God Made Me and You*, is a book for every family bookshelf. This colorful, poetic presentation of ethnic diversity shouts the truth of God's creative design as found in Scripture. *God Made Me and You* is more than a storybook, it is a teaching tool designed to bring a biblical worldview of humankind into your living room."
Marty Machowski, Family Pastor at Covenant Fellowship Church, Glen Mills, PA; author of *The Ology*, *Long Story Short*, and other gospel-centered resources for church and home

"The rhythm of words and the magic of rhyme will open your child's eyes to the beauty of race in God's good design. In *God Made Me and You*, Shai Linne has created a masterpiece of biblical truth that your child will love and that all of us need. I look forward to reading it with my own family. It's the perfect gift to spread the unifying message that Jesus brings to our divided culture."

Champ Thornton, Pastor; author of *The Radical Book for Kids* and *Pass It On: A Proverbs Journal for the Next Generation*

"Shai Linne is a pastor at heart. And it shows on every page as he brings all of his talent as a theological wordsmith to bear on this simple story of God's delightfully diverse design. Get this book to remind yourself and the little ones you love of the glorious message of Jesus that is bringing together people from every tribe and tongue."

Dan DeWitt, Associate Professor of Applied Theology and Apologetics at Cedarville University; director of the Center for Biblical Apologetics and Public Christianity; author of *Life in the Wild*

"This is a wonderful resource for teaching our children about God's heart for the nations. Shai rightly reminds us that we are all united in Adam and that we ought to rejoice in 'saints of all colors.' Diversity, rightly understood, is not a PC slogan; it's a biblical hope and expectation. I'm excited to share this book with my own kids."

Kevin DeYoung, Senior Pastor, Christ Covenant Church, Matthews, NC; Assistant Professor of Systematic Theology, Reformed Theological Seminary; author of *The Biggest Story*

"Oh, what a difference it would make if every family would pick up this book and take to heart its message, starting at a young age! This is biblical theology for kids—and all of us!—on God's beautiful design of ethnicity, as winsomely told and displayed through creative and faithful artist-theologians. I recommend it with great gratitude and enthusiasm!"

Justin Taylor, Managing Editor, *ESV Study Bible*

"Thoughtfully written and whimsically illustrated, this resource will help children (and those who love and lead them) learn to identify thinking and behavior that diminish humans made in the image of God, see ethnic and other differences through gospel eyes, and celebrate the diversity he has created for his glory."

Nancy DeMoss Wolgemuth, Author; teacher; host of *Revive Our Hearts*

"Shai Linne has given us a beautiful story that will not only captivate little hearts and minds, it will help parents clearly explain biblical reasons for why we can and should celebrate God's design for ethnic diversity. But don't think the story is all Linne has for you—read the back to be inspired to continue the conversation when the book is closed. Well done!"

Trillia Newbell, Author of the kids' book *God's Very Good Idea: A True Story of God's Delightfully Different Family*